little book of

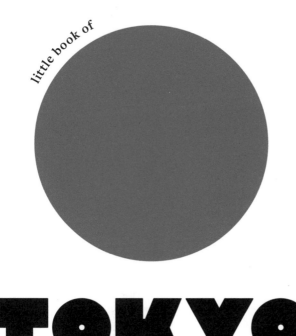

TOKYO
style

Published in 2023 by Welbeck
An imprint of Welbeck Non-Fiction Limited
part of Welbeck Publishing Group
Offices in: London – 20 Mortimer Street, London W1T 3JW &
Sydney – 205 Commonwealth Street, Surry Hills 2010
www.welbeckpublishing.com

ISBN 978-1-80279-497-7

Printed in Spain

10 9 8 7 6 5 4 3 2 1

EMMANUELLE DIRIX

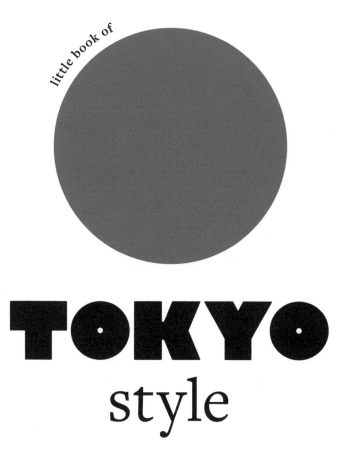

little book of

TOKYO
style

W
WELBECK

CONTENTS

introduction page 6

iNTRODUCTiON

"The fashions that have swept in from the East represent a totally different attitude towards how clothes should look."
The *New York Times*, November 14, 1982

These days Tokyo is a well-established fixture on the fashion map, and the term "Japanese fashion" evokes a strong image. At the top end of the market, Japanese designers remain synonymous with avant-garde design; at the affordable end, companies such as Uniqlo and MUJI bring high-quality, utilitarian design to the masses. Japanese streetwear brands have a global cult following owing to their innovative cut and use of materials, and Japanese subcultures introduced the world to kawaii (the aesthetic of cute).

This worldwide recognition and popularity is often regarded as a fairly recent phenomenon. In the early 1980s, two Japanese designers' debut made waves on the Parisian catwalks and were quickly credited by the press with establishing Japanese fashion. Rei Kawakubo and Yohji Yamamoto undoubtedly set out a unique and, more importantly, different aesthetic to the looks dominating the European and American catwalks at the time, and it's also true that the ensuing press attention helped to spread

Washed broad blouse, MUJI 2022.

and popularize the idea of Japanese fashion worldwide. However, it is not accurate to see the 1980s as the start of Japanese fashion. To do so ignores both Japan's rich fashion history and the successful endeavours both at home and abroad of the Japanese fashion designers who preceded the "deconstructive" duo of Yamamoto and Kawakubo.

As this book will set out, Japan has always been a nation with a thriving fashion culture that has seen the creation of unique styles and aesthetics often based on inherently Japanese concepts and ideas.

So why do so many still think of Japanese fashion as a fairly recent invention? The key question here is: *How do we define fashion?* All too often the answer is still from the moment when the West becomes aware of a particular style, and embraces (if not appropriates) it – hence the frequent citation of the 1980s as the birth of Japanese fashion.

Equally, what is recognized as fashion is often limited. For far too long "traditional" garments such as the kimono were categorized as ethnic and thus static, often viewed as costume as opposed to fashion. Indigenous garments, particularly non-Western clothing, were therefore almost by definition overlooked. And yet, as we'll see, Japan has had a strong and unique fashion culture for centuries.

This book will trace the key moments in the development of Japanese fashion, discuss its impact on Western fashion, take a closer look at the ethos and work of key designers, and celebrate the uniqueness of Japanese street styles.

Two Yohji Yamamoto silhouettes with details from traditional Japanese paintings on a marbled ground, Spring/Summer 1987.

Above: Street style reminiscent of the Crows, shot at the
Rakuten Autumn/Winter Fashion Week Tokyo, 2021.

Opposite: An early pleated silhouette by Issey Miyake, from
Spring/Summer 1989. In 1993 he would launch his Pleats
Please line entirely focused on pleated garments.

chapter 1

FRAMING THE KIMONO

The kimono is an iconic item of dress and closely wrapped up, if not synonymous with, Japanese identity and dress. What we know as the kimono has been worn in Japan by all classes of society and by both sexes since the late sixteenth century but, as Anna Jackson observed in *Kimono: The Art and Evolution of Japanese Fashion*, "the fact that its basic shape has remained consistent over the centuries, means that the kimono is often viewed as a simple, timeless garment" and therefore excluded from fashion.

This view says more about the Western-centric nature of fashion studies than the kimono. In the West, as Elizabeth Wilson points out in *Adorned in Dreams*, fashion is often defined as "dress in which the key feature is rapid and continual changing of styles". By contrast, the basic shape of the kimono, a straight-seamed garment constructed with minimal cutting from a single bolt of cloth, has not changed for centuries. However, to conflate this with the notion that the garment was excluded from fashion culture could not be more misleading.

Western fashion understands change as a shift in the silhouette to accentuate ever shifting erogenous zones, but in Japanese style the body is essentially irrelevant. Meaning, as well as fashionability, does not lie with the garment itself but with its surface.

An eighteenth-century embroidered and hand-painted kosode, the short-sleeved predecessor of the kimono.

An eighteenth-century woodblock print depicting an act from
Suzuki Harunobu's play *Sekidera Komachi*, about Ono no Komachi,
the great ninth-century poet also known for her beauty.

Kimonos came in different quality fabrics, with different patterns and embellishments depending on the wearer's wealth and social status. Like Western fashion it thus identified the owner's position in society. For commoners, the kimono was made of cotton with simple patterns, was mostly functional, and was not changed or replaced with a regularity defined by changing aesthetics. At the top end of the social hierarchy, however, richly decorated silk kimonos were the haute couture of their day and came in endless designs and colours. Several kimonos might be layered to reveal contrasting patterns and these could in turn be combined with patterned obis (the wide belt worn to wear the kimono in a closed manner). The result was an outfit that was anything but simple to wear.

Just as in Europe where patterns and colours changed, so did those of kimonos; Japanese dress culture had its own fashion cycle that dictated regular change, as evidenced by surviving kimonos in museum collections worldwide. The variety, craftsmanship, originality and quality of these luxury kimonos is akin to what was being worn in the upper echelons of European court society. Indeed, the kimono did not go unnoticed by privileged European society: after the Dutch brought the kimono to Europe, it had a significant impact on the informal dress culture of the social elite, and kimono-inspired garments became a status symbol to show off the wearer's wealth, taste and style.

The country's closed borders meant that few Japanese-made kimonos were available outside the country, but after Japan opened up for trade in the mid-nineteenth century a veritable wave of Japanomania swept the West. Warehouses sold imported Japanese goods, including textiles, inspiring a fashion for the wearing of kimonos in the drawing rooms of London and Paris, and also exerting a significant influence on European interiors – further proof that Japanese design was in fact extremely fashionable.

La Liseuse, by Georges Croegaert, 1888. The interior reflects the European Japonisme craze of the second half of the nineteenth century following Japan's opening up to foreign trade.

A summer kimono, made of silk gauze and treated by Tsutsugaki (a technique of resist dyeing in which rice paste is used to create the design). From the first quarter of the twentieth century.

The liberation of Western fashion

The popularity of Japanese products remained strong well into the early years of the twentieth century. But aside from the West's adoption of Japanese styles as an expression of fashion, it is also important to understand the central role that the kimono played in the seismic shifts in Western female fashion which marked the late nineteenth and early twentieth centuries. It is no overstatement to say that the kimono significantly contributed to the liberation of the female wardrobe.

Many French haute couturiers, upmarket London dressmakers and department stores on both sides of the Atlantic enthusiastically incorporated Japanese "elements" into their designs, including crane and blossom embroideries, obi-style belts and parasols decorated with bold "Japanese" patterns. However, it is the impact of traditional Japanese pattern cutting and the Japanese approach to the human body that was of real importance in this period and a major catalyst for change.

In Japanese dress the shape of the body is irrelevant. The kimono is an assemblage of rectangular pieces of fabric, and unless worn, it lies flat. This means that the body itself gives the garment shape, which as a dressmaking ethos is the diametric opposite to Western tailoring, which has historically been concerned with shaping the body. Through Western eyes, the kimono may therefore be perceived as shapeless and loose fitting. To Japanese eyes, by contrast, the superfluous space created between the body and the garment is referred to as *ma*: "a rich space that possesses incalculable energy" according to Akiko Fukai in *Future Beauty*.

Kimonos To Paris

Photograph from the early twentieth century of a European kimono coat embroidered with cranes, attributed to the couturier Paul Poiret.

Pochoir print from *Gazette du Bon Ton* showing Paul Poiret's
1913 "Sorbet" evening ensemble featuring his lampshade
tunic with kosode-inspired sleeves and obi-style belt.

Pochoir print from *Gazette du Bon Ton* showing a Paul Poiret
wrap dress with kimono-inspired collar and sleeves.

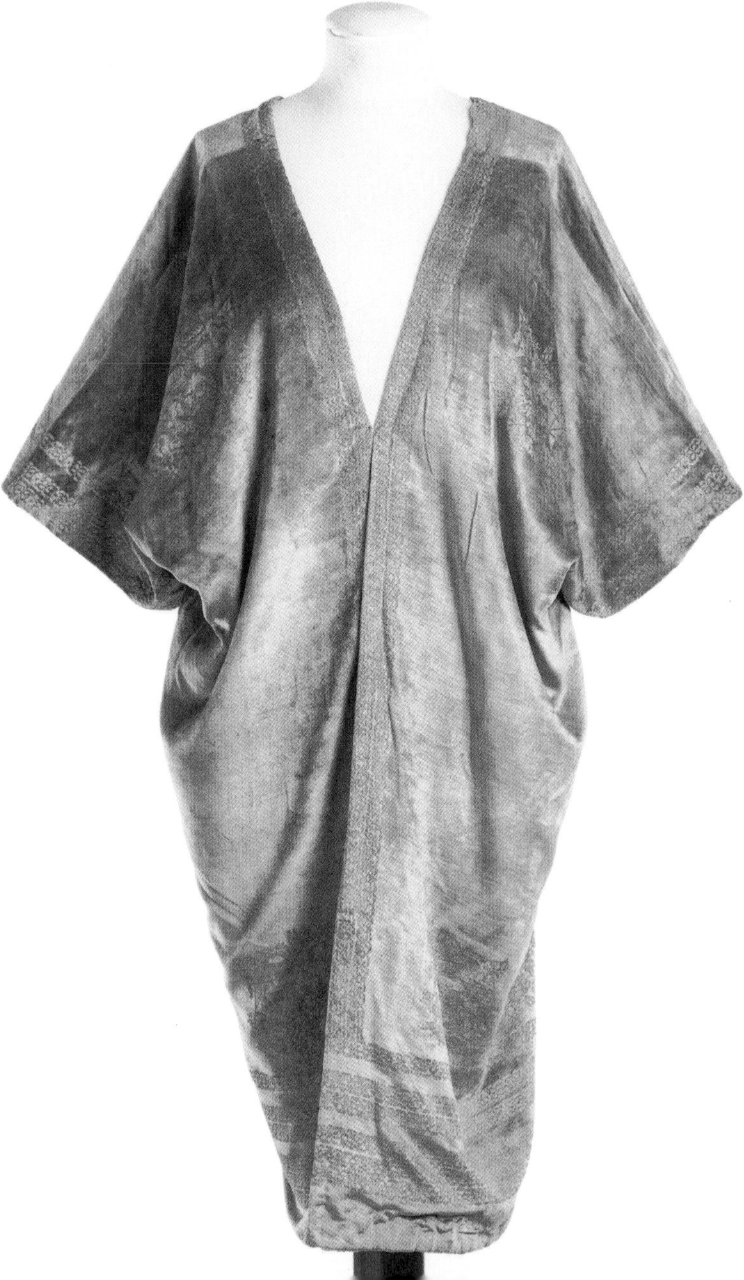

Compared to contemporary European fashions that relied on the corset, the kimono was incredibly comfortable, which in part explains its popularity as domestic wear. And it was this comfortable interplay between garment and body that made the structure of the kimono so attractive to dress reformers and progressive fashion designers alike. Indeed, the late nineteenth and early twentieth century was a time when antique and regional dress types were studied and incorporated into Western dress to revolutionize shape: most notably the Greek chiton, the North African and Middle Eastern kaftan, and the kimono.

Very quickly the kimono's structure became the starting point from which fashionable but comfortable womenswear could originate. Many see it as a clear influence on the tea gown of the late nineteenth century, and in the early twentieth century it inspired haute couturiers to create more comfortable women's fashions. In Paris Paul Poiret and the Callot Soeurs designed a significant number of silhouettes that were clearly derived from the kimono; in Italy, Mariano Fortuny teamed his flat Delphos dresses with kimono-inspired coats.

Even after the Japonisme craze waned, and the over-the-top "Oriental" designs fell out of fashion, the influence of the kimono remained evident in the work, and specifically in the patterns, of some of fashion's greatest innovators, including Madeleine Vionnet, Charles James and Cristóbal Balenciaga.

Silk velvet embroidered evening coat by Mariano Fortuny c.1925. While the embroidery is of Coptic origin, the T-shaped garment resembles the silhouette of the kimono which remained a popular reference in high fashion, albeit increasingly less literal, into the 1930s.

Above: Illustration of the evening ensemble "Feleurs de Japon" (Japanese Flower) by Callot Soeurs, 1914.

Opposite: Photograph of a model wearing a Madeleine Vionnet ensemble with kimono-inspired collar and belt, c.1922.

chapter 2

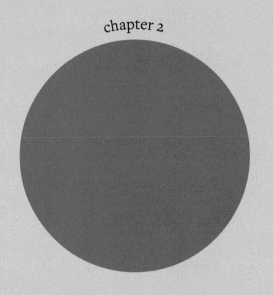

JAPAN
ON THE
GLOBAL
STAGE

SHiFTiNG JAPANESE FASHiONS

While Japan had had a thriving fashion culture before it opened up to Western trade in the mid-nineteenth century, its new position on the global stage introduced significant changes.

Western dress had its most immediate impact on the Imperial court and specifically on men's dress. From the 1870s the Emperor dressed in European-style military costume, and formal Western clothes became increasingly worn for official engagements and ceremonies. Some women from the elite also adopted Western dress for formal occasions, and Western handbags became popular, but mostly women continued to wear the kimono. That is not to say that they were oblivious to Western fashion, just that they chose to engage with it on their terms. For example, women in Japan were just as susceptible to "Perkin's Purple", one of the first synthetic dyes, which became a worldwide sensation in 1856. Women everywhere now dressed in purple, and purple kimonos became all the rage, thus showing that Japanese women were happy to use European inventions to suit local styles. The kimono increasingly became a garment that embodied Japanese national identity, specifically female Japanese identity, and its association with nationalism goes a long way to explain its enduring popularity and uptake even after men mostly abandoned it.

Blossoming Cherry Trees in Ueno Park – polychrome woodblock print from 1888, depicting the Imperial couple dressed in fashionable Western silhouette.

Japan On The Global Stage

Above: Photograph of two *moga*, or "modern girls", dressed in fashionable Western dress on the streets of Tokyo in the early 1930s.

Opposite: An early nineteenth-century woman's kosode – silk embroidered with a design of wisteria, symbolizing love and longevity in Japanese culture.

Above: An advert featuring a fashionable street scene for
Japanese cosmetics brand Shiseido from 1927.

Opposite: A woodblock print by Torii Kotondo from 1929
featuring a woman in a kimono with an art deco style design,
highlighting the stylistic union of tradition and modernity.

Japan On The Global Stage

By the 1920s the streets of Tokyo saw women in modern
Western dress, though the majority still donned kimonos.
While the cut remained unchanged, these interwar kimonos
were anything but traditional. They came in bold modern
prints: art deco motifs were particularly popular, not least
because they could be scaled up easily to make for arresting
designs. These bold and bright kimonos were styled with
thoroughly modern accessories such as gloves, fur stoles and
fringed shawls, and some women wore their obi across the
chest to achieve a silhouette similar to the ones presented at
the couture houses in Paris.

All these examples were clear evidence of the Western influence on Japanese society and aesthetics, but it is worth stressing this was no simple adoption of Western beauty ideals, let alone a cultural takeover as witnessed in many colonies at this point. Instead it showed that the Japanese could confidently pick and choose elements of Western culture to incorporate into their own culture in a way that worked for them. This is a point we'll return to when looking at more contemporary Japanese designers and indeed Japanese subcultural styles.

Above: Costume design by Charles Ricketts for an unidentified female chorus member in *The Mikado*, performed at the Prince's Theatre in London, 1926.

Opposite: A photograph, c. 1924, of a modern Japanese *moga* in a fashionable Western-style sack dress, pictured in front of the Café Tiger in Shinjuku Tokyo. Shinjuku became increasingly popular with young fashionable men and women, but was considered vulgar by more traditional, older people for its booming Western café scene.

These gloriously modern kimonos were the height of fashion, but history also teaches us that they were the garment's last hurrah. The impact of the Pacific War (1941–45) and the subsequent impact on Japanese national identity goes a long way to explain the dramatic decrease in the wearing of the kimono in the second half of the twentieth century. It remained, and indeed remains, a ceremonial garment worn at key events – mostly in a woman's life these days – but it is no longer the favoured daywear. It has undergone something of a revival of late (see Chapter 8), but the second half of the twentieth century saw Japan turn into a hyper technologically

Above: A Tokyo street scene c.1950. While the men are dressed in Western three-piece suits, the women wear kimonos and obis made of fine silk.

Opposite: Pedestrians strolling down a shopping street in Tokyo's Ginza district in the late 1930s.

advanced nation (even viewed as quasi futuristic by many),
and like countries across the globe its people increasingly
favoured a global uniform that was mostly Western in origin.

But while the West was changing Japanese styles, Japanese
designers also started making their mark on Western fashion.
The first to do so was Hanae Mori, best known as simply
Mori. She opened her fashion house Hiyoshiya in 1951
and went on to design hundreds of costumes for Japanese
films. In 1965 she showed her East Meets West fashion
collection in New York, and by 1977 she was admitted into
Paris's prestigious Chambre Syndicale de la Haute Couture,
couture's official governing body. Mori's designs took
Western fashion as their reference but remained "perfumed
with Japanese spirit" – as Suzy Menkes wrote in 2001. Mori
herself attributed her design approach to how she worked
in the early years of her house. At that time the wives of
the American occupying forces would bring her clothes to
sew, and she was fascinated by how they would wrap fabric
around themselves to study their silhouette from all angles.
These experiences set her on a specific design course that
saw her master Western cutting and sewing techniques and
pursue an aesthetic that Barbara Vinken described in *Future
Beauty* as "more Parisian than the Parisians" (p. 34). By
doing so, Mori challenged the French monopoly on elegance.
Her work is often overlooked because she did not present
overtly avant-garde silhouettes like those who followed in her
footsteps, but she nevertheless went to Paris to challenge.
The fact that her house was the first led by an Asian woman
to be recognized as an official haute couture house is an
exceptional achievement and indeed one that paved the way
for other Asian designers.

Model Hiroko wearing a Hanae Mori chiffon dress that fuses traditional
Japanese prints and cuts with fashionable Western hippie aesthetics, 1972.

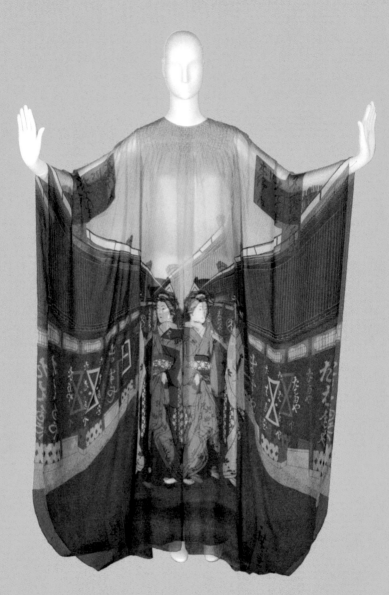

Silk chiffon evening dress by Hanae Mori from 1974
with updated traditional Japanese designs.

Dress by Hanae Mori from 1973 featuring a modern interpretation of kimono sleeves and a traditional cherry blossom design.

chapter 3

THE
1970S

JAPAN TAKES PARiS

Mori may have been the only Japanese designer who was a member of the Chambre Syndicale de la Haute Couture, but she was not the only Japanese designer in Paris during the 1970s.

In 1970 Kenzo Takada opened his first clothing store in the city, controversially called Jungle Jap. Kenzo had trained at Tokyo's famous Bunka Fashion College and worked for a Japanese department store before moving to Paris in 1965. The first five years in the city he worked both as a freelance designer selling sketches to fashion houses and as a stylist at a textile manufacturer.

His goal was to open his own boutique, and a chance meeting at a market in 1970 saw him renting a small shop in the Galerie Vivienne in Paris's 2nd arrondissement. Inspired by the painter Henri Rousseau, he decorated the shop with jungle-inspired murals featuring colourful lilies and figures surrounded by cheetahs. Later his love for Rousseau's art would lead him to use the tiger from his painting *Le Rêve* as the inspiration for his label's logo.

His first collection was made for $200 and was an eclectic mix of colours and patterns which he showed at the Galerie Vivienne. He was soon picked up by the fashion world and in the same year *Elle* featured one of his designs on their cover.

The 1970s

Kenzo Takada surrounded by models dressed in his 1976 Winter collection photographed in his Parisian JAP boutique on the Passage Choiseul.

A year later he showed both in Tokyo and New York. In 1973 he took the then popular peasant style (think Laura Ashley/ Gunne Sax) and added volume and loosened the silhouette. This intervention not only led a silhouette change in fashion, it also cemented his reputation for fantasy folklore looks in bright patterned colours and helped him gain a loyal and growing following. By the close of 1976 he opened his flagship store Kenzo, and his brand went from strength to strength throughout the 1970s and '80s, his bright, playful designs perfectly aligning with the predominant fashion zeitgeist.

Kenzo was not the only Japanese man with dreams of fashion to land in Paris in 1965. Issey Miyake arrived in the city that year, too, in his case to attend the École de la Chambre de la Couture Parisienne. Unlike Kenzo he did not found his label in the city; indeed after working for Guy Laroche and then Givenchy, he moved to New York, returning in 1970 to Tokyo to set up his design studio to produce high-end women's fashion.

That year Japan hosted Expo '70, the first world's fair to be held in the country. One of the largest expositions in history, it was a significant moment: for the first time since the post-war occupation and Americanization of the country, Japan was starting to carve out a modern identity, which accommodated both native and Western ideas and traditions. It is within this context that Miyake's work needs to be considered.

While he did not wish to be categorized as a Japanese designer, given the "exotic" associations that continued in the 1970s, his early worked repeatedly featured *sashiko,* a stitched quilted cotton worn by Japanese peasants, as well as reinterpretations of Japanese fisherman tunics and peasant dress. But it was not necessarily their Japanese-ness that interested him: rather he was fascinated by shape and form, which became increasingly apparent over the next decade.

Takada Kenzo in his Parisian showroom, c. 1973.

Above: Kansai Yamamoto (centre) and Issey Miyake
(right) preparing for a joint fashion show at the National
Olympic Memorial Youth Centre in Tokyo, 1974.

Opposite: Models at Issey Miyake's show for
Spring/Summer 1975, held in Paris.

His experimentations with shape were matched by his fascination and research into materials. Miyake closely collaborated with a host of textile technologists to explore the possibilities offered by new synthetic materials, but his work always balanced the old with the new, the traditional with the technological – a point worth emphasizing. For example, he visited historic crafts regions and worked to revitalize traditional production and dye techniques that were on the verge of extinction, trying to find new uses for traditional methods. Indeed, he received worldwide acclaim for his efforts to incorporate modern technology with traditional techniques.

In 1973 Miyake started presenting his collections in Paris, and quickly gained much respect from the international fashion press and buyers alike. By 1975 he had opened his first Parisian boutique. A year later he launched his concept A Piece of Cloth, which wrapped the body in a single length of fabric, thereby suggesting a modern take on *ma* in the form of flat two-dimensional clothing. Once again, he combined

Above: A nylon bathing outfit in red, violet and green panels with tassled hood, Issey Miyake, 1979.

Opposite: At Issey Miyake's Autumn/Winter show 1979–80, held in Paris, this model wears a wrap-over jumpsuit with subtle nods to the designer's Japanese heritage.

Above: Model Marie Helvin wearing a cotton
kimono by Kansai Yamamoto, 1971.

Opposite: Oversized Kansai Yamamoto cape dress with a graphic
design inspired by traditional kabuki performers, 1971.

the traditional with the modern – in this instance, a concept fundamental to Japanese dress used to create modern, intelligent fashion.

While Miyake was lauded for his experiments with materials, Kansai Yamamoto, another Bunka Fashion College graduate, was making headlines for very different reasons. Kansai had opened his first Tokyo boutique in 1968 and by 1971 he'd opened his own company: Yamamoto Kansai Company Ltd. In the same year he showed both in the US and London, and his international debut collection – a mix of sculptural shapes, clashing textures and prints in technicolour – attracted plenty of industry attention. *Harpers & Queen* magazine put his work on the cover, with the line "Explosion from Tokyo, the fantastic sculpture clothes of a fashion architect" (July 1971).

Following his London show, a collaboration with David Bowie emerged. Kansai was commissioned to create the wardrobe for Bowie's Ziggy Stardust stage persona: brightly printed kimonos, colourful knitted bodysuits, and possibly most famous of all a striped balloon jumpsuit. Their collaboration continued for several more years both on and off stage and his success led to him showing in Paris in 1975 and opening his first boutique in the city two years later.

Kansai was rarely described as a Japanese designer, probably because his brightly coloured designs contrasted sharply with the sober deconstructive silhouettes of what the 1980s came to define as Japanese fashion, but his silhouettes and colour palette were nonetheless directly influenced by kabuki costumes and the art of the Japanese Momoyama period (1573–1615). His bold designs can also be seen as an expression of the Japanese concept of *basara*: a love of flamboyance. And it was this trademark flamboyance in Kansai's work that saw his continued success into the next decade.

But while Kenzo, Kansai and Miyake were making a name for themselves on the international stage, at home in Japan other key players were busy at work. In 1972 Yohji Yamamoto, who had graduated from Bunka a few years previously, established his own fashion label. A year later Rei Kawakubo, who unlike her male counterparts had no formal fashion training, founded her label Comme des Garçons. By the late 1970s both were showing their collections in Tokyo, expanding their operations and biding their time to take Paris and the world by storm.

Model Caroline Coon wears white platform boots and a red-and-white, hand-knitted woollen jumpsuit by Kansai Yamamoto.

Above: David Bowie during a costume fitting session with Kansai Yamamoto ahead of his performance in Tokyo, 1973.

Opposite: David Bowie performing in a mini kimono commissioned from Kansai Yamamoto, 1973.

chapter 4

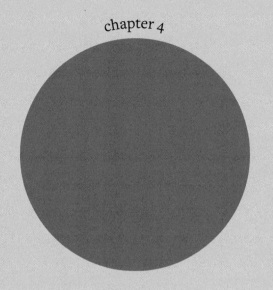

THE
1980S
REVOLUTION

REWRiTiNG THE CANON

Historically fashion has been very much discussed from a Western-centric perspective, meaning that something would be formally accepted into "the canon" only after it had been labelled as Fashion with a capital F by Western journalists, cultural critics or even academics.

As the previous chapters have shown, Japanese fashion culture had been thriving inside Japan for centuries, continually pushed forward by the upper echelons of society just as it had been in Europe.

Japanese fashion designers had also established successful international careers in the post-war era, and the press made reference to their origins now and then. However, possibly due to the lack of unifying design characteristics of the different players, or the absence of an explicit "Japanese-ness" in their collective work, there was no discussion as yet of such a thing as "Japanese Fashion".

All that was about to change, and the wider world, who often still associated Japanese design with tradition and kimonos, was about to dramatically revise that (incorrect) opinion.

The spring/summer 1984 défilés, held in Paris in the autumn of 1982, are commonly seen as the start date of the Japanese

The 1980s Revolution

Issey Miyake's show for Spring/Summer 1986, held in Paris.

Revolution, as the press has referred to it since. This was the fashion week when Rei Kawakubo (as Comme des Garçons) and Yohji Yamamoto showed what many at the time described as "apocalyptic" collections.

Both had in fact made their Parisian debut the previous year but neither was a member of the Fédération française de la couture, du prêt-à-porter des couturiers et des créateurs de mode, so their shows had been attended by only a handful of people and very few press representatives. An exception was a journalist for the French newspaper *Libération* who was one of the first outside of Japan to cover the duo's work. He remarked, rightly so, on the key features of their designs: an emphasis on form, material possibilities and deconstruction.

By the spring of the following year, both designers had joined the Fédération and were added to the official show calendar, and their shows have never gone unnoticed since.

Their first collections hit like a bomb – and many critics literally compared them to that. Kawakubo, whose collection was aptly but also shockingly named Destroy, sent models down the runway in black jumpers deliberately knitted with "mistakes" to create holes, asymmetric dresses with drawstrings and voluminous artfully ripped and unravelled skirts, creased and patchworked dresses that looked threadbare, T-shirts that had been picked apart and resewn, skirts assembled from "scrap" fabrics with missing panels. The models also walked out to flashing lights, with dishevelled hair and deliberately messed-up make-up, marching down the runway with vacant expressions ... the antithesis of the elegant, fun-loving woman who dominated the rest of Paris fashion week.

Rei Kawakubo/Comme des Garçons distressed-effect shirt dress, formed from pieced cotton patches with intentional holes, c. 1983.

The 1980s Revolution

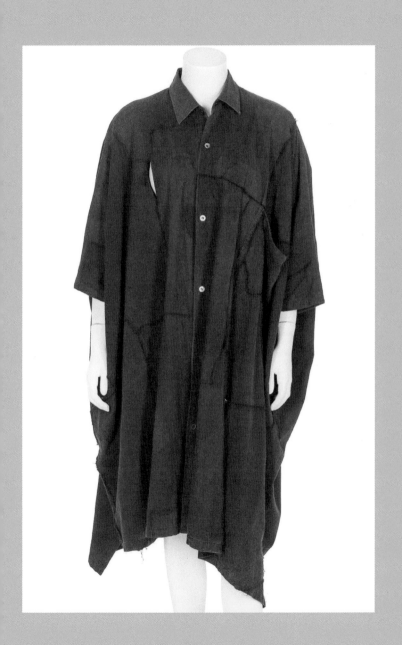

Yamamoto's show similarly included asymmetrical, voluminous, distressed and deconstructed garments, and his models' styling equally challenged the accepted beauty ideals of high fashion; his work was labelled the "beggar's look" by more conservative news outlets.

Several journalists considered the collections too shocking and different and expressed their discomfort at the spectacle they had witnessed in their reporting. *Le Figaro* suggested Kawakubo's clothes looked as if they would be worn by nuclear holocaust survivors – this, apparently, was "Hiroshima chic" – and Yamamoto's clothes were said to look as if they had been bombed to shreds.

The predominant hue of both collections was black, which for some journalists only added to the menacing overall feel. At the time the colour was not particularly fashionable on Western catwalks and was mostly associated with street and subcultures. This excessive use of black only reinforced their reservations about the clothes, though others were more positive: in November 1983, French *Vogue* compared them to "calligraphy scrolls which symbolize a beauty devoid of colour".

Le Figaro may have labelled their work as "not fit to be worn" by their readers, but progressive journalists and, more importantly, fashion buyers appreciated the originality and new direction they offered.

By the spring of the following year Comme des Garçons and Yamamoto's collections were available in fashionable boutiques throughout Europe and the United States, including prestigious Parisian department stores.

Comme des Garçons, Autumn/Winter 1983.

EAST MEETS WEST

Today voluminous, asymmetric and deconstructed garments are part of the fashion lexicon, and available at all ends of the market. These initial designs deserve some closer attention, not only to appreciate the truly seismic impact of the Japanese designers on fashion, but also to understand their frame of reference and how they introduced Europe and America to new Eastern ideas about aesthetics and ornamentation.

It must be stressed that the ideas they embodied did not fit the narrow view the West still held about the East. Western Orientalism, a naïve understanding of the East shaped by colonial dominance and heavily reliant on exotic and negative stereotypes, was still very much alive in the 1980s. *Opium*, Yves Saint Laurent's power fragrance launched in 1977, is a perfect example. Its name and the accompanying adverts from the 1970s and '80s perfectly illustrate the mix of exoticism, stereotyping and cultural ignorance still applied to non-Western cultures.

This limited and stereotypical understanding of other cultures' history and heritage meant many of the profoundly Japanese ideas, references and concepts present in the early collections by Yamamoto and Kawakubo (and, to an extent, Miyake) were at best entirely missed and at worst categorized as aggressive or ugly, clothes for ragpickers and beggars.

A cream Yohji Yamamoto crinkled and knotted cotton jersey ensemble made up of a stockinette dress, a cotton jersey combination trouser/dress and a matching jacket. Spring/Summer, 1983.

The 1980s Revolution

The more informed journalists linked the torn, frayed, ragged clothes of those first collections to the collective Japanese trauma of Hiroshima. Both designers were toddlers when the atom bomb was dropped and were undoubtedly influenced by its cultural fallout and impact on Japanese identity. However, this is a limited interpretation, and one that focuses very much on the surface and misses something more conceptual that underpins much of Japanese design.

The concepts of *wabi* – without decoration or visible and/or explicit luxury – and *sabi* – something old and atmospheric – together constitute *wabi-sabi*, a world view that centres on transience and imperfection. The concept finds its origin in Buddhism, but over time its expression has developed into a specifically Japanese aesthetic concept and sensibility. Aesthetic characteristics of *wabi-sabi* include asymmetry, roughness, imperfection, incompletion, modesty and austerity. This concept affects every Japanese art form – and fashion was and is no exception. The Edo merchant culture of the seventeenth and eighteenth centuries shunned extravagance in clothes and instead elevated what is best regarded as shabby refinement. Similarly, *sashiko* stitching finds its origins in the peasantry of ancient Japan. *Sashiko* roughly translates as "little stabs" and the technique was used to mend fabrics, extending their life at the same time as embellishing. In fact, it was the imperfect nature of these folk textiles that created much cultural appreciation.

The idea of *wabi-sabi* and its expression in textile practices therefore offers an interpretation of the clothes presented by Yamamoto and Kawakubo which is more philosophical and conceptual, and less literal.

Wrapped ensemble from Yohji Yamamoto's Spring/Summer 1986 show, held in Paris.

The 1980s Revolution

Above: A Yohji Yamamoto black cutwork, cotton kimono jacket, c. 1985.

Opposite: Two voluminous silhouettes from the Comme des Garçons show for Spring/Summer 1984, held in Paris.

A moulded acrylic breastplate/bustier from Issey Miyake's
collection for Autumn/Winter 1980–81.

The Japanese concept of *ma* – the space created between the
body and the garment (see Chapter 1) – is closely associated
with the kimono, and can also shed further light on these
early collections. Unlike Western fashions, the kimono is
essentially a flat piece of clothing that needs the body to
animate it and to give it shape. Kawakubo, Yamamoto and
Miyake's garments would take on their final form only
once worn. Only on the body do these three-dimensional

creations, which hang off the wearer, reveal their full structural complexity.

This entirely new, arguably sensitive, approach to fashion quickly brought success to the Japanese designers, including Miyake, whose experiments by the 1980s had become increasingly conceptual and made use of wire, bamboo, rattan, paper and plastic. All three designers soon became favourites of those who preferred something that was more avant-garde, timeless and experimental, and which offered a true alternative to what had hitherto been presented by high fashion. Their sales and popularity increased year on year, and so did their cultural standing. Though all three designers – but in particular Kawakubo – remained to some extent seen as fashion agitators, the press quickly became supportive and celebrated their difference.

By the mid-1980s, Japanese fashion was an established concept that evoked a clear image. It had broken new ground and it presented an innovative set of construction techniques, a conceptual approach to shape, and progressive methods in pattern cutting, while also reawakening a love affair with the colour black.

In fewer than five years its importance and impact had become indisputable, widening the definition of fashion, if not changing its course. Japanese fashion's conceptual influence could clearly be seen in the work of several of the Antwerp Six, a group of young Belgian designers who burst onto the fashion scene in 1986.

The remainder of the decade saw an ever-growing interest in the world of Japanese designers, not just from fashion but also from the performing arts, cinema and the art world. Miyake, who had made the cover of the prestigious publication *Artforum* in 1982, was celebrated the following

Above: Two ensembles from Yohji Yamamoto's
Autumn/Winter 1986–87 collection.

Opposite: Model wearing Yohji Yamamoto's Z-shaped,
belted jacket and long, knife-pleated skirt, c. 1987.

year by the Stedelijk Museum Amsterdam with the exhibition
Issey Miyake: Bodyworks; Kawakubo published a book of
photographs featuring work by Peter Lindbergh in 1986; and
in 1989 Yamamoto collaborated with cult cinematographer
Wim Wenders on the documentary *Notebook on Cities and
Clothes*, commissioned by the Centre Pompidou in Paris.

In less than 10 years, Japanese fashion had conquered the
world, and the next decade would see it continue to shock,
amaze and challenge.

chapter 5

1980S TOKYO STYLE

WEST MEETS EAST

During the 1980s Japanese designers were busy changing the world of high fashion by shaking up the catwalks of Paris and London, but fashion in Japan itself was also rapidly changing. Tokyo was the country's fashion capital and where the decade's numerous fashionable looks and different style tribes could be seen converging on the streets.

The 1980s was Japan's Golden Age and witnessed the consolidation of the opportunities and technological advances of the previous decades to create a world power. The economy was booming and the country, riding on this wave of optimism and no longer overshadowed by post-war occupation and debts, was busy carving out a modern Japanese identity.

This new direction and identity struck a balance between the local and the global: it adopted Western ideals and ideas and integrated these with Japanese traditions and values.

This was also reflected in the decade's fashion culture, which saw Japan's adoption of various Western styles – not in a passive way, but rather by making them their own and giving them a decidedly Japanese twist.

Street or style culture was a fairly recent phenomenon in Japan, having only really emerged in the latter part of the

Two young women wearing leopard-print ensembles, Tokyo 1987.

1970s. At that time young people in Tokyo (just like their contemporaries in London) renounced the values of previous generations, and this was reflected in their style choices. Early Tokyo street fashion is therefore associated with confrontation, just like the punk styles of the late 1970s in London.

By the start of the 1980s, however, a strong economy and a world-leading consumer society changed the outlook of a younger generation, and an appreciation and adoption of the "adult" lifestyle sees the popularity of styles both preppy and *nyutora* (new traditional). The new traditional styles had various iterations, but all at their core involved the adoption of Western styles: the *ita-kaji*, which translates as "Italian casual", favoured casual Mediterranean styles, while Shibuya casual (or Shibukaji, after one of the most popular shopping and entertainment districts of Tokyo) blended French elegance with more casual wear.

The most popular of all the new traditional styles, however, was the preppy look. This had emerged in the United States in the early twentieth century, and was widespread by the 1950s. Its name derives from the private, preparatory schools attended by the children of the financial elite in preparation for an Ivy League education. The look was symbolic of the privileged leisure class, and was introduced to Japan by Kensuke Ishizu and his label Van Jacket in the early 1960s. Its popularization, both as a brand and a look, was not immediate, but the economic comfort of the 1980s, paired with a revival of the look in America itself, saw preppy and Ivy styles become a major fashion on the streets of first Tokyo and later other Japanese cities. Blazers, button-down shirts, Bermuda shorts, sports coats, sweaters with the name of Ivy league universities, and cardigans, in navy, grey and

1980s Tokyo Style

A couple dressed in preppy styles, Tokyo 1984.

Above: Young dancers in Harajuku, Tokyo 1982. Their fashions show the dominant American influence on Japanese styles in the 1980s.

Opposite: A couple in Shibuya casual, or Shibukaji, fashions posing for photographs, Tokyo 1989.

cream, by brands such as Lacoste and Ralph Lauren were de rigueur for young fashionable Tokyoites. The look was predominantly influential on men's fashion, but some women adopted it, too, by wearing knee-length skirts paired with high socks, and blazers or cardigans worn over crisp white blouses or college sweaters. To learn about the preppy look, men could consult magazines such as *Popeye* and *JJ* while women had *An-An* and *CanCam* magazines.

Magazines and books were instrumental in the dissemination of styles throughout the Japan of the 1980s and '90s, and each style tribe had its own publication(s) that promoted its target audience's chosen looks, informed them about the "right" brands, and served as style guides, breaking down all the different elements and informing their readers where to purchase the items. These magazines were not only very modern and ahead of their time compared to many of their Western counterparts: they were also an expression of the strength of the Japanese consumer economy.

Another iteration of the popularity of more traditional and/or mature styles was the emergence and subsequent popularity of the Bodikon style in the mid-1980s. This style also centred on the adoption of Western fashion and brands, in particular Hervé Léger which, alongside Alaïa and Mugler, was one of the Parisian pioneers of body-con designs. The look started off as quite conservative if not demure: mono-coloured, figure-hugging dresses were paired with matching jackets, expensive designer handbags and scarves, and the look was finished off with a pair of sensible court shoes. Within a few years, though, it had shed most of its respectability and become increasingly sexualized. Now, instead of daywear it became mostly associated with club culture.

Music culture played an important part in the promotion and dissemination of specific sartorial styles during the 1980s and this was also the case in Japan. In the UK *The Face* and *i-D* magazines blended music and fashion reporting, and in Japan music magazines aimed at promoting different genres also featured style sections alongside music coverage. An early but popular music style was the Kote Kei look, which blended elements of new wave, punk and glam rock. Its followers had

A young woman in Bodikon fashion, Tokyo 1987.

big backcombed hair and wore leather and studded garments. While they wore lots of black, they should not be confused with the Karasu-zoku or the Group of Crows.

The Crows were predominantly women who dressed in all black outfits and tried to emulate Yamamoto and Kawakubo's offerings that were causing a stir on the other side of the world. Those who could afford them proudly wore original Comme pieces; others bought local brands who offered their own versions of the voluminous, asymmetrical and deconstructed silhouettes. It's argued that the Karasu-zoku culture represented a symbolic revolt against, if not a rejection of, the traditional concept of the devoted Japanese housewife. Interestingly, the Western press at the time accused Kawakubo of making genderless clothes – which did not accentuate traditional erogenous zones and instead shrouded the body in an interplay of fabric and space – so Japanese women adopting these silhouettes to reject traditional gender roles and expectations, affirmed their subversive potential.

The Crows shared some visual and conceptual ideas with other subcultures, most notably punk and the New Romantics, but their origin and popularity is very much attributed to Yamamoto and Kawakubo. This does not negate the Crows' relationship to international subcultures, nor does it make theirs an exclusively home-grown style. But Kawakubo and Yamamoto had themselves been inspired by Western street, club and subcultures including punk and goth. The Crows were therefore a perfect example that showed fashion could no longer be traced to one clear point of origin but instead was a constantly evolving cultural expression that saw different groups borrow from

1980s Tokyo Style

A young punk, Tokyo 1986.

Two teens dressed in casual American fashions, Tokyo 1986.

Two female Crows dressed top to toe in black genderless outfits, Tokyo 1982.

one another. This exchange was pushing fashion forward, perfectly mixing the global with the local.

The final Tokyo street style that needs examining is the Otome or Maiden look, which became popular in the early years of the decade. Otome style is heavily indebted to *Olive* magazine, which first appeared in 1982 as a general women's fashion magazine, but which was relaunched a year later under the creative direction of Tsumori Chisato, who introduced a whole new focus on a distinctly romantic, feminine look. Otome style blended Eastern and Western influences, and mixed historic styles with contemporary colour palettes and prints. Defining features included circle and A-line skirts, cardigans, and blouses with big bows or lace collars, all in soft hues or featuring vintage-style floral prints, the whole teamed with either flat Mary Janes or tassel loafers. The Japanese brand Pink House was the most popular retailer of the style and featured heavily on the pages of *Olive*.

The Otome look was a huge hit with schoolgirls and women in their early twenties. The fashion projected a cute, girly and innocent if not infantilized image, which was mirrored in comic and manga cartoon characters of the decade, and was also adopted by popular female Japanese TV and music stars. The style's cultural importance resides in the fact that it can be seen as the precursor to Lolita styles of the 1990s, which would see Japanese street culture go global.

The 1980s witnessed a plethora of Tokyo street styles, all of which were influenced by and included Western elements. Soon, though, the tables would be turned, and street and subcultures across the world would be looking towards certain Tokyo districts for fashion guidance: *kawaii* culture was about to conquer the world.

Model wearing black suit at Yohji Yamamoto's Autumn/Winter 1988–89 show.

Above: A girl dressed in Otome style by Pink House,
photographed for *Olive* magazine, 1984.

Opposite: A young woman roller-skating on the streets of Tokyo, 1981.

chapter 6

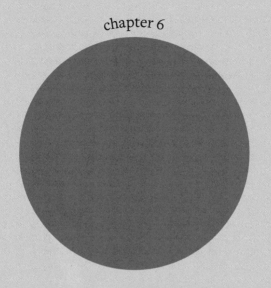

THE
1990S

EXPLORATIONS IN FABRIC

By the 1990s the ideas introduced by Japanese designers had become accepted by Western fashion culture and were exerting significant influence, being adopted by a host of new young designers.

The predominant aesthetic direction of the 1990s was more than in part set in motion by Kawakubo, Miyake and Yamamoto in the previous decade. The minimalism that dominated high-end fashion for the first half of the 1990s (and to an extent the ugly/shock chic that emerged in the second half) is arguably an adoption and interpretation of the stripped-down, deconstructed aesthetic that they introduced. Designers such as Helmut Lang, Jil Sander and Calvin Klein now rejected the excess of the 1980s – the bright colours, bold prints and over-the-top embellishments – in favour of subdued tones, austere cuts and an emphasis on concept over luxury and excess, a change that cannot be explained by the decade's economic downturn alone. Sure, economies in trouble have always witnessed directional changes in fashion, but in this case the choice of that direction and the aesthetic characteristics cannot be separated from the looks and concepts introduced by the Japanese contingency.

Explorations into the beauty of imperfection and conceptual cuts were pushed by Helmut Lang; innovative use of

A model displays a Pleats Please reversible square cape and pants ensemble as part of Issey Miyake's Autumn/Winter 1995 collection, shown in Paris.

materials and modesty punctuated the work of Prada; asymmetry and volume play was discernible in the work of Ann Demeulemeester; conceptual experimentation and deconstructivism were central to the collections of Martin Margiela and later Alexander McQueen. All were concerned with redefining notions of beauty, luxury and taste, and as had happened to their Japanese predecessors, their work was often initially received with misunderstanding, shock or outrage but quickly became influential and celebrated.

The wider interpretation and adoption of their aesthetic ideas did not mean Kawakubo et al. no longer stood out. Far from it. All three remained at the forefront of avant-garde fashion, their collections evidencing their continual growth and development as designers and their commitment to exploring the boundaries of the body, materials, shape and beauty. The 1990s sees all three develop their own specific direction that sets them on a focused design trajectory.

From the outset of his career Issey Miyake had not only designed clothes but also created the fabrics from which they were made. His extensive knowledge of traditional weaving and dye techniques was combined with the technical capabilities of the manufacturers of synthetic fibres to develop original and futuristic textiles. In the second half of the '80s his polyester fabrics were attracting worldwide attention, not least because he was one of the first to elevate man-made materials to luxury status. The culmination of his fabric research and development came in 1993 with the launch of his revolutionary line Pleats Please. To achieve their architectural shapes, the clothes were first cut and sewn together from fabric several times larger than the finished item, and subsequently hand-fed into a pleating machine.

A Yohji Yamamoto "Bustle" ensemble, Autumn/Winter 1995–96.

These synthetic pleated garments were not only revolutionary in terms of production, they were also different because they were more democratically priced than most designer wear, they could be rolled into coils that were easy to pack, they were machine washable (almost all luxury fashion was still dry clean only) and they would always miraculously "bounce" back into shape.

His search for new concepts and modes of production did not stop there. For his next major innovation, he returned to one of his original concepts: what can be achieved with a single length of cloth, a very Japanese idea that is fundamental to the design of the kimono. His 1976 concept A Piece of Cloth became the basis for the development of a new production process that made fully finished garments without the need for sewing. His A-POC line was unveiled in 1999 and consisted of a range of tubular knitwear made without machine sewn seams and finished on a roll. The wearer, who was deliberately integrated into the production process, was required to cut along the marked lines of the knitted tube to "release" the garments embedded into the fabric. Both Pleats Please and A-POC received worldwide acclaim.

Yamamoto's work too remained very focused on material, but in his case the intimate relationship between fabric and body was central. He continued his love affair with black throughout the 1990s and his dominant use of the colour was, as stated in *Future Beauty: 30 Years of Japanese Fashion,* "intended to focus the viewer's attention on cut and proportion with no distraction". His work became increasingly abstract, if not sculptural at times, but always remained comfortable. It also evidenced his incredible pattern and tailoring skills, and more than once his skills were

The 1990s

Yohji Yamamoto black ready-to-wear hoop dress, Autumn/Winter 1990–91.

compared to one of the most influential and talented haute couturiers of the twentieth century, Cristóbal Balenciaga. Though many stressed the Japanese influences of his clothes, it would be incorrect to ignore his incredible knowledge of Western fashion and tailoring, and he often made reference to, or developed his own take on, classic silhouettes.

Like Miyake, Kawakubo experimented extensively with fabrics throughout the decade and, like Yamamoto, pushed the limits of the relationship between the body, fabric and form, albeit in a very different, some would say more explicit, manner. Her output in the 1990s can be seen as both an in-depth exploration and a development of her early ideas. Conceptual design remains central to her work but, as with Yamamoto, it would be wrong to ignore her extensive knowledge and understanding of Western fashion. She is often accused of rejecting or deconstructing Western norms of beauty, but we must not forget that this implies an inherent understanding of those norms: you cannot successfully reject what you do not understand. Her 1995 collection Sweeter than Sweet saw models wearing pastel-coloured dresses with bustle-like tubes and voluminous tulle skirts that evoked nineteenth-century crinolines, so drawing attention to the artificiality and restrictive nature of historic Western silhouettes. Her most subversive engagement with this theme of fashion and artificiality came in her 1997 collection Dress Meets Body, Body Meets Dress, often colloquially referred to as the Lumps and Bumps collection. The clothes presented completely distorted the natural shape of the body through padded inserts (again a reference to fashions of the eighteenth and nineteenth centuries). These were used to distort instead of enhance and in so doing they completely freed the body from its own boundaries.

Silhouette from Comme des Garçons' 1995 Autumn/Winter Sweeter than Sweet collection intended to challenge feminine stereotypes.

Above: Pieces from the Body Meets Dress, Dress Meets Body collection worn by mixed-gender performers for a collaboration between Kawakubo and choreographer Merce Cunningham. The silhouettes intend to question what exactly is a woman.

Opposite: A gingham dress stuffed with lumpen filler to create a new silhouette, from the Comme des Garçons 1997 collection Body Meets Dress, Dress Meets Body – often referred to as the "lumps and bumps" show.

The 1990s

This more extreme anatomical distortion, pared with an interest in techno-textiles, was also a feature of the work of newcomer Junya Watanabe. Watanabe joined Comme des Garçons upon graduating from Bunka in 1984, where he became responsible for the brand's Tricot line. Quickly becoming Kawakubo's protégé, he launched his own label as part of Comme in 1992. His 1990s collections showed his hallmark mix of reworked classic cuts in unexpected materials. His references to fashion's history evidenced that, like his predecessors, he had a thorough understanding of classic shapes and proportions, but equally like the others his work was never just a simple reference. From Victorian undergarments to mid-century subcultural styles, he made them his own through an innovative use of materials and unique tailoring techniques. His 2000 collection Techno Couture, which featured his iconic honeycomb ruffs, capes and dresses in bright colours, was hailed as the pinnacle of futuristic fashion despite the obvious references to Elizabethan fashions.

This play with historic references was not limited to Japanese designers, but their take on history was complex and understated in contrast to the dark luxury and excess seen in the work of the likes of Galliano and McQueen.

Japan continued to occupy an enviable place on the international luxury fashion stage, but at home things were more complex, and this complexity was of course expressed in Tokyo fashions.

The 1990s

Junya Watanabe layered ensemble with obi style belt worn across the chest.

chapter 7

1990S TOKYO STYLE

TOKYO GOES GLOBAL

The 1980s had seen Japan conquer the global fashion stage and become a world-leading modern nation. This Golden Age was, however, short-lived. In 1991 the speculative bubble burst and the economic stagnation began.

Initially, the change in economic fortune did not alter the course of Tokyo fashion. In fact, a desire to hang onto the glories of the previous decade meant there was a continuation in popularity of Western styles interpreted to suit local tastes and needs. The two most popular examples were Shibuya casual and French casual. The former was a blend of the preppy and Bodikon style mixed with a Japanese interpretation of Bon Chic Bon Genre (the conservative, classic style of the French monied classes), the latter a more casual look that relied heavily on brands like agnès b. and classic French pieces such as striped T-shirts, beige trenches and relaxed blazers.

These two smart-casual looks remained popular with a general audience for much of the decade. It's the Tokyo street styles and subcultures, many closely linked to specific districts of the city, that deserve closer attention because it is there that we find not only true fashion innovation but also a clearer reaction to the shifts in Japanese society which resulted from the deepening economic crisis. It would be impossible to discuss all the style and subcultures of the decade, let alone their subgroups – many were very short-

Young women in Shibuya casual style, Tokyo 1991.

1990s Tokyo Style

lived and had very specific local variations – so instead we will focus on the main style directions and the unique and/or innovating fashions.

Music and cinema remained the main importers of Western popular culture, including fashion. This was especially true for men's fashions, and arguably the most dramatic shift in Tokyo style was brought about through its embracing of US hip-hop culture. The first cultural entrepreneur to bring hip-

Woman dressed in French casual style, Tokyo 1992.

hop back to Japan was musician and DJ Hiroshi Fujiwara, who first came into contact with the New York music scene in the 1980s. He is credited with driving the import of hip-hop, rap, breakdance, graffiti and urban clothing styles. He was also one of the founding fathers of the Urahara scene – short for Ura-Harajuku, an area of a few blocks between the Tokyo districts of Harajuku and Aoyama, which in the 1990s became a street-style Mecca. In 1990 he founded his brand Good Enough. Just over a decade later his status as a pioneer of streetwear and global trendsetter was confirmed in 2002 with Nike's HTM line (Hiroshi, Tinker and Mark) and in 2008 with Levi's, for the cult Japan-only line Fenom.

By the mid-'90s, the streets of Ura were lined with a plethora of boutiques, all with their own distinct style focus but all selling what is best defined as streetwear. Street fashions from the United Kingdom or the United States; vintage Levi's jeans; skatewear and BMX clothing; and local interpretations of global subcultural and music fashions.

On April 1, 1993, the now cult boutique NOWHERE opened. The brainchild of Jun Takahashi and Nigo, it was the first to stock cult brands like Undercover and BAPE (Bathing Ape). Its uniquely curated stock, which was mostly sourced from the US and included a mix of new designs, vintage items and deadstock trainers, ensured its legendary status in the global history of streetwear until this day.

Throughout the decade and beyond, it remained the mecca of streetwear, and stocked influential brands including AFFA (Anarchy Forever Forever Anarchy), co-designed by Jun Takahashi and Hiroshi Fujiwara and presenting a 1990s interpretation of 1970s punk styles; Forty Percent Against Rights (FPAR) and its bold DIY graphic text T-shirts; and Shinsuke Takizawa's T-shirt and denim brand NEIGHBORHOOD.

The varying aesthetics and subcultural influences of the different brands show just how eclectic Japanese streetwear was, and while we use the term universally, it is important to stress the mix-and-match approach to its Japanese expression.

NOWHERE quickly became *the* place to shop and be seen, where Japanese celebrities and schoolkids alike stocked up on streetwear. But it wasn't just schoolkids who adopted

2月号 増刊 通巻7号 1996年2月1日発行

STREET 2月号増刊号

No ⁷

フルーツ

No.7

500yen

interview

アリス

アウ

仙

原宿

フリースタイル

Above: Cover of *FRUiTs* magazine, No. 7, 1997. The street-style publication is hailed for introducing the world to the varied and unique fashion styles of Harajuku.

Opposite: Young man in hip-hop inspired outfit mixing items from Japanese cult labels AFFA and Good Enough, c. 1998.

streetwear: young men in their twenties could also be seen sporting streetwear ensembles. Today this is a common sight, but at the time it was an expression of rebellion by young Japanese men (and women) against the increasing oppressive demands of Japanese corporate culture, and the high expectations and enormous social pressure put on people to succeed from a young age. These pressures were not new but they were arguably intensified by the uncertain economic climate of the decade, and this for the first time led to many young people reluctant to conform.

The 1970s had seen *Sukebans* – literally "delinquent girls", the name for schoolgirl gangs who had public fights and behaved in a socially unacceptable manner, but these were the exception not the rule. The rebellion phenomenon of the 1990s, however, was much more extensive.

While streetwear remained the favoured rebellious style for men throughout the majority of the decade, for women the second half of the decade saw the emergence of a new subculture trend: Gyaru, an umbrella term for the different interpretations of American schoolgirl styles. This collection of looks all represented a form of non-compliance, if not rebellion, against traditional female roles, and the press was quick to label these girls as delinquents, rebels and prostitutes. At the least shocking end of the Gyaru spectrum, we find the Kogal "little girl", who wore her schoolgirl uniform with a very short skirt and loose legwarmer socks as a fashion statement, and the Paragal (Paradise Girl), who sported looks inspired by Californian casual fashions as seen on the TV show *Baywatch*, which was broadcast in Japan in the second half of the decade.

Two teenage girls, one in plain clothes (left) and the other sporting the typical Kogal look of a high-school uniform paired with slouch socks. Tokyo 1997.

FRUiTS magazine, No. 1, 1997. The cover features two teenagers dressed in cyberpunk styles and childlike DIY accessories, capturing the mix-and-match approach to style of Harajuku youth.

The transition from the Kogal via the Paragal to the Ganguro (burn black look) happened in the mid-1990s and came about through the popularization of hair bleaching and (fake) tanned skin. The underlying idea was one of rebellion against traditional Japanese beauty ideals – natural beauty, dark hair and pale skin – and thus traditional femininity.

Paragal girls had mostly favoured fairly natural make-up and hair styles, but the Ganguro sported a very dark (fake) tan, further enhanced by bleached and/or dyed hair (in shades of bright orange, shocking pink or platinum blonde), and excessively applied white eye make-up and pale pearly lipstick. The look was finished off with long false lashes, black eyeliner and liberally applied face jewels. They wore brightly coloured clothes and a plethora of accessories. Their looks were documented in and influenced by *Egg* magazine, which became the main reference for Shibuya street-style photography once it launched in 1995.

Ganguro ultimately was a fairly short-lived fashion and like many street styles morphed into different looks, although we can trace a direct line to the Yamanba and Manba styles of the 2000s.

When discussing Japanese street style, it is impossible to avoid mentioning the impact of technology. In the 1990s Japan tried to soften the economic blow by focusing on its technological export market. Owing to this, two brands in particular became global household names: Nintendo and Sony, especially because of their new gaming technology. Not only were these brands vital to the financial survival and recovery of the economy, they also introduced a much wider audience to gaming and manga culture and thus anime styles.

1990s Tokyo Style

By the second half of the decade, it was fairly common for teenagers to have mobile phones, and the integration of technology into everyday life contributed to the rise of cyber fashions, whose adopters favoured materials with an artificial appearance such as wet-look vinyl, plastics, synthetic velour or faux fur. Stylistically there were parallels with manga styles through the use of the bright colours and futuristic cuts and accessories, and several subgenres were spawned, most famously cyberpunk, which remains popular until this day.

Girls looking for something more reserved sought inspiration in the 1980s' Otome style and the J-rock (Japanese rock) scene and Visual kei (which had evolved out of the Kote Kei scene discussed in Chapter 5). The combination of the two birthed the now iconic Lolita look, which became synonymous with Harajuku. Often misunderstood, the style bore no relationship to Nabokov nor the sexual deviance central to his book. Instead, inspired by romantic rococo colour palettes and Victorian cuts, the look was meant to represent childish innocence and naivety, values in stark contrast to the social expectations placed on Japanese girls and women. So, despite its *kawaii* (cute) character, this look can therefore also be interpreted as a form of sartorial resistance. The style was heavily promoted in, and indeed globally disseminated, by Shoichi Aoki's now legendary *FRUiTS* magazine.

Like many of the other street styles, Lolita is a stylistic genre with many subcategories, but what unites all of them is obsessive attention to detail and the high quality of the clothes and accessories. Brands such as Pink House, Milk and Pretty were some of the main early retailers of the style, but many young women who could not afford these excessively priced garments taught themselves to sew, and so the style also had a thriving DIY culture, something traditionally associated with punk subcultures.

Cover of *FRUiTS* magazine, No. 13, 1998. This carefully curated mishmash of brightly coloured clothes and jewellery became known as Decora, an aesthetic that revolved around an excessive amount of accessories, especially plastic hair accessories and bracelets.

1990s Tokyo Style

One of the first variations was Gothic Lolita, who instead of pastel hues and feminine shapes, favoured more austerely tailored, dark clothing and make-up. By contrast, the sweet Lolita took *kawaii* to new heights through an adoption of childlike if not childish themes in dress, including sweets, cupcakes and baby animals, and items such as large bows or headbands, all in the style of *Alice in Wonderland*. The overall feel was one of a Little Girl Lost.

Punk Lolita teamed black baby doll dresses with striped tights and chunky black boots; Country Lolita wore *Little House on the Prairie*-style dresses and straw hats; Sailor and Pirate Lolita played about with nautical themes; Guro Lolita incorporated horror elements such as bandages and fake blood; and Oji Lolita was a style worn by Lolita's male counterpart, but many girls also adopted the look of tailored trousers and top hats. These cute girlish styles were mostly worn by schoolgirls and university students, but this should not negate their rebellious quality: the 1980s Maiden had been solely about a classic, demure cuteness, while Lolita was a far more complex and political style and subculture that used sartorial escapism to engage with a hyper-capitalist society, which its members wished to avoid joining.

The Lolita style, largely through its depiction in *FRUiTS*, was sent around the globe and became synonymous with Tokyo fashion. Its popularity can be measured in just how many Western pop stars, celebrities and indeed designers incorporated elements of the look in their work, if not fully appropriating it. Even Kawakubo has given several stylistic nods to the Lolita in her collections over the years, though naturally always in a conceptual, intellectual manner.

Overleaf: Teenagers in Crow and punk fashions, Harajuku 1997.

Japanese teenage girls dressed in Sweet Lolita styles,
Harajuku 2019. The Sweet Lolita look tends to favour
light and pastel colours and child-like accessories.

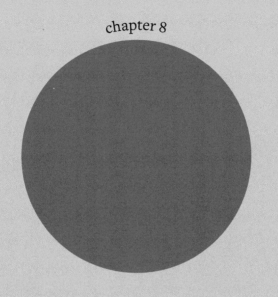

chapter 8

2000S - PRESENT

TOKYO'S SUPER MIX

Today fashion is a global phenomenon: high streets the world over are populated with the same brands and chain stores; social media platforms have complemented if not taken over the role of the traditional fashion media in disseminating trends, and they do so in seconds as opposed to weeks or months; and the same images are accessible across the globe.

Since the early 2000s these new ways of disseminating fashion, coupled with the rise of celebrity culture, have led many to believe there is no longer such a thing as "local" fashion.

Globalization has indeed seen a homogenization of style, with people across the globe wearing similar fashion "uniforms". However, one of globalization's more unexpected consequences has been the rise of localization – the process of making something local – and in this Tokyo remains a leader. In fact, arguably it has always been ahead of the curve, adopting Western styles but infusing them with local colour since the late 1960s – and this is arguably key to its continued relevance in and to fashion culture.

Another consequence of globalization and the rise of online culture is the death of authentic subcultures and, by extension subcultural, styles. While it's not the purpose of this book to explore this, what we can say and show with certainty is that Tokyo's fashion districts have not seen the disappearance of unique youth street styles which continue to influence mainstream trends both in and outside of Japan.

Cover of *FRUiTS* magazine, No. 30, 1999.

Above: A model wearing the Japanese brand pays des fées. The toy accents and pearl trim headpiece show how Harajuku street styles have bubbled up into high fashion.

Opposite: A guest during at Rakuten Fashion Week Tokyo 2021 wearing a Charles Jeffrey Loverboy outfit reminiscent of earlier DIY Harajuku fashions.

In fact, Japanese street fashion has had a monumental influence on the fashion industry in the past two decades: the same social media that is often held responsible for the death of street styles in the West has allowed Japanese street fashions to become widely known, adopted and admired the world over. Established fashion media heavyweights such as *Vogue* and a host of influential international fashion blogs have dissected and celebrated Tokyo's unique fashion character: a perfect blend of popular culture with traditional local aesthetics.

2000s – Present

Unisex style

The end of the 1990s saw the Urahara street style, initially led and adopted by young men, become popular with women. Although elaborately tailored and detailed Lolita costumes in endless variety continued to occupy one end of the fashion spectrum, the other end saw a growing popularity in boyish styles of denim jeans, trainers, sweatshirts and relaxed T-shirts. This extension of the style to women in the early 2000s developed into a wider trend for unisex – or what today we more appropriately refer to as genderless – fashion. Here specifically meaning separates often derived from the male wardrobe but executed in darker and/or neutral shades that avoid overly feminine shapes and detailing and which prioritize cut and quality over more showy elements. This continues to remain popular with large sections of the market.

But to merely see the emergence of this style as a morphing of one trend into another would mean missing some important factors that contributed to this understated yet hugely important stylistic shift.

The 2000s is not only the moment when fashion goes global through the advent of Web 2.0. It is also the moment when a new way of communicating helps to break down generational divides and does away to a large extent with earlier ideas about age-appropriate fashion, thereby opening up the fashion market to a much wider audience. In addition, in Tokyo this is exactly the time that sees the generational maturation of its early street-style pioneers, who were not about to abandon their commitment to fashion and

2000s – Present

A guest during the Amazon Tokyo Fashion Week 2018, dressed in a contemporary street-style outfit.

Above left: A guest during the Amazon Tokyo Fashion Week 2018, dressed in a contemporary street-style outfit.

Above right: A street-style shot of a woman in a Uniqlo Lumelu Dress, Ann Demeulemeester shoes and a MSPC (Master Piece) bag, showcasing a contemporary mix of local and global street styles, Tokyo 2016.

style purely because of age. Their styles matured but they continued to set trends and keep their finger on the fashion/style pulse, an important factor that needs acknowledging when examining the rise of the fashionable but less showy unisex style.

In Japan the retail chain Uniqlo was instrumental in retailing the look. Uniqlo dates back to 1949. The company underwent several name and directional changes in its long history but in the 1980s started shaping its contemporary retail identity when it opened a unisex casual-wear store. In the late 1990s the company underwent yet more market repositioning changes which resulted in the opening of their first urban Uniqlo store in Tokyo's Harajuku district, a move that boldly stated their intention to be part of a fashion-forward scene. Their affordable, high quality, well-cut separates have made Uniqlo the global go-to brand for understated genderless styles.

Of course, there is also a global context to the unisex fashion that one cannot ignore. The 1990s experiments with unisex looks (think Jil Sander, Helmut Lang and Calvin Klein, among others) had by the early 2000s gone mainstream and been adopted into the Western fashion canon, so this style was not limited to the streets of Tokyo. So while we cannot argue that the unisex trend, which has come to dominate all echelons of the fashion system over the past two decades, was a strictly Japanese invention, the country played a defining role in its dissemination and has been central to its popularity.

This issue of origin in many ways is irrelevant as a discussion, not least because Tokyo street styles have always taken global trends and put an original spin on them. Instead of focusing on who originated what – authorship being a very Western concern – it is more interesting to focus on that local customization. If fashion is increasingly homogenous, then surely the devil is in the local detail?

The mid to late 2000s saw the emergence of what can broadly be termed celebrity style, fuelled by the new cultural role of celebrity and paparazzi culture, and shaped by new publications both on- and offline detailing the every move of particular stars. This led to, for example, the global craze for towelling tracksuits à la Juicy Couture which were seen on young women around the globe, and Tokyo was no exception. However, due to the extreme differences between the LA and Tokyo beauty ideal, this global look was styled in a distinctly Japanese manner that stripped it of many of its original connotations.

In Tokyo these predominantly American celebrity styles, mixed with the heightened popularity of It bags and designer shoes in the early 2000s, led to what became known as Gal-mix (sometimes referred to as Celeb-Kei), or the mixing of fast-fashion brands teamed with designer accessories to "elevate" the look.

Agejo, a street style that was arguably a subset or an offshoot of Gal-mix, emerged in 2007 and prioritized fashionability and appearance over brands. The emergence of Agejo style is no mere coincidence or simple evolving of Gal-mix; its emergence is perfectly aligned with the introduction of many Western fast-fashion brands such as H&M onto the Tokyo fashion landscape. Within a few short years fast fashion in Japan, as elsewhere, became widespread and dominated the consumer landscape. Together with digital culture these fast-fashion chains were instrumental in creating what fashion journalist and critic Ted Polhemus called the Supermarket of Style, the contemporary world where all of history is up for grabs to be perpetually recombined into "new" styles. Stylistically it means endless referencing (either through vintage and retro originals or new fast-fashion copies), but it is also the death of true subcultures and a weakening of a commitment to one style in favour of a post-modern mix.

A young Japanese Shiro Lolita, a Lolita style made up entirely of white/cream/off-white clothing. Harajuku 2009.

In cities like London, this led to the hyper-commercialization of traditional subcultural spaces like Camden Town – and, in so doing, wiping out much of its uniqueness – but in Japan this cut-and-paste approach was in essence nothing new. Possibly this explains how Tokyo street culture managed to avoid the sterile homogenization of this period, while its seasoned adeptness at putting a specific local spin on global

Teenager sporting contemporary Super Mix make-up
and hairstyle, which draws from and mixes various street
and subcultural aesthetics into a new, original look.

styles now singled it out as a fashion leader in an era where
many observers accepted that authenticity and originality
were mostly dead and buried.

Consequently, in the 2010s the Tokyo street style scene saw
endless combinations, deconstructions and reconstructions
of previous styles into new ones: the boyish Urahara street
styles, Gyaru schoolgirl looks (see Chapter 7) and konsaba,
a conservative style that itself had developed out of Otome
and French-style (see Chapter 5), combined into a feminine
look that was both *kawaii* and mainstream enough to be

accessible for all; Otome met forest pixie via 1970s' Prairie dresses to create Mori Kei (arguably a source of inspiration for the cottage-core aesthetic); Dolly Kei saw an eclectic mix of European medieval peasant dress, Romani embellishments and detailing, and fairy tale styles; Cult Party Kei mixed Christian religious symbols with '90s anime looks in pastel shades… the variety was endless and the past a never-ending source of inspiration.

As these cross-fertilized styles became so complex, and drew inspiration from so many different sources and aesthetics, *ACROSS* magazine coined the term Super Mix style to try and describe and analyze these new street fashions. They were quick to point out that Super Mix was not its own type or kei, but instead described the blurring of styles and trend, which has become near impossible to categorize but has remained most certainly novel and fashionable.

Super Mix style drew inspiration from a wide variety of sources, and the gathering and mixing of the clothing was approached in a similar manner: so fast-fashion, vintage (which saw a huge surge in popularity), high-end designer, independent boutique and home-made items were combined to achieve these often complex, multidimensional looks.

Interestingly the complexity and fast-paced change of fashion styles in Tokyo had one, somewhat unexpected, consequence that brings us full circle. The incessant changes, the increasingly homogenized global styles and the indisputable continuing Western dominance of fashion culture have combined with this re-examining of vintage and retro styles to lead the revival of the kimono as a fashion garment. A growing number of young women are re-exploring the garment, buying both vintage and new kimonos. New brands such as Mamechiyo Modern, Rumi Rock, Iroca and Modern Antenna all look for individual ways to engage with Japan's

Above: Young woman in a mix of Sweet and
Country Lolita styles, Shibuya 2014.

Opposite: Young woman wearing an alternatively styled kimono
paired with contemporary tabi shoes and carrying a traditional
Japanese taiko wadaiko drum. Rakuten Fashion Week Tokyo 2022.

2000s – Present

history and traditions and make these relevant for a new
generation and a new world, fusing the local with the global.

And this perhaps is, and always has been, the strength and
unique quality of Japanese style and Tokyo street fashions:
the ability to make the global local, and the local global, and
to take inspiration from the past and turn it into the future.
Qualities that ensure its enduring reputation and status as a
true style centre.

chapter 9

TOKYO'S INFLUENCE ON THE WORLD

THE NEW WAVE

To trace the contribution of Japanese designers to the global fashion scene since 2000 means, by definition, making difficult choices: so many influential, talented and innovating individuals and brands have made their mark not just on fashion but also on product design, styling and retailing.

In addition to these new design voices, the early pioneers have remained relevant, and their work, ethos and methods continue to inspire fashion students and designers across the globe. The recent passing of both Issey Miyake and Hanae Mori elicited an outpouring of praise not just for their designs but for their trailblazing and continuous relevance, a hard thing to achieve in an industry obsessed with endless turnover and the ever illusive New.

The variety of designers and styles that have emerged in the past two decades to join the original line-up of Japanese Greats is extensive and sadly impossible to cover. This diversity has been showcased and celebrated at Tokyo Fashion Week since 2005 and today in excess of 50 brands participate, covering anything from urban streetwear to luxury contemporary kimonos.

The introduction of a Tokyo Fashion Week has not diminished Japanese designers being represented on international catwalks, however, and while they now span

A model walks the runway during Chitose Abe's Spring/Summer 2017 show for Sacai, held in Paris.

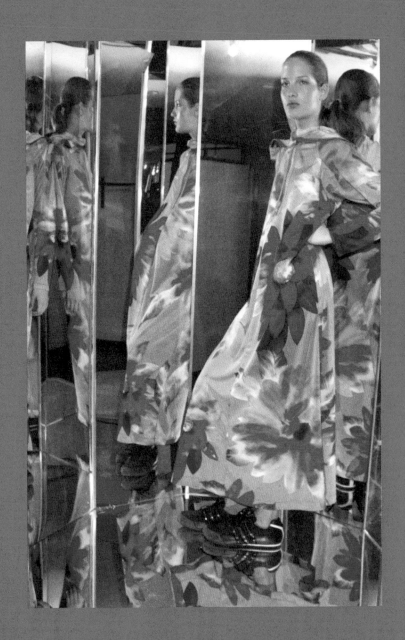

a wide aesthetic spectrum, they share many fundamental approaches and methods with their spiritual fashion forefathers: an interest in traditional Japanese craft techniques, the development of new textile shapes and/or materials, and a fusion of Japanese concepts with Western stylistic history to achieve original and innovative outcomes.

Arguably the most important international change that has occurred during recent years is a shift in recognition and status. As we have seen, Japanese designers have long occupied a respected position within fashion as highly influential pioneers of avant-garde design, but they were not household names and their reach was often limited to the elitist ranks of high fashion. In the early years of the twenty-first century, this was about to change.

In 2003 two designers would attract immense press attention and praise for their new fashion collaborations and introduce a younger generation to, and renew a global interest in, Japanese fashion design. That year saw the launch of Y-3, the now cult brand collaboration between Yohji Yamamoto and Adidas which married high-end conceptual fashion with streetwear, anticipating the future of luxury fashion. Yamamoto suggested the collaboration, keen to find new ways to rejuvenate fashion which he felt had become staid and to engage young people and elicit a renewed excitement in design. Y-3 was met with critical acclaim and financial success soon followed, too. Indeed, it became the measuring stick for industry collaborations and it set the bar very high.

Another Japanese artist/designer who was elevated that year to the status of pop and fashion culture hero, especially for a young audience, was Takashi Murakami. Marc Jacobs, then

Model wearing a Y-3 Adidas floral dress and sneakers by Yohji Yamamoto, 2003.

creative director at Louis Vuitton, engaged him to redesign the brand's monogram collection, which he did in his brightly coloured palette. His bags became an instant hit and were seen on the arm of every celebrity in town. Other equally recognizable and successful collections soon followed. His colourful pop-py designs made Louis Vuitton relevant and extremely desirable to a new, younger clientele.

Aside from accessory design, Murakami was also invited to take charge of the visual merchandizing for several Louis Vuitton flagship stores, setting out a blueprint for artist and fashion collaborations. The collaboration continued for 12 years, an exceedingly long time in fashion, evidencing just how lucrative it was, and was only terminated when Marc Jacobs was replaced.

But while these high-profile collaborations might have occupied the majority of column inches, and indeed helped nurture a mainstream interest in Japanese design, many other creatives were also busy making their mark on the international fashion stage.

In 1999, Chitose Abe, after training at Comme and Watanabe, launched her brand Sacai. She quickly became known for her designs, inspired by Tokyo's bustling street culture and fusing intricate sportswear and delicate tailoring. She stated early on that Japanese-ness was not a design tendency that she focused on in her work, but the technical complexity and ability demonstrated in the silhouettes, the combination of contrasting textiles, and her play with 3D design all hint at a sensitivity she shares with other Japanese designers. Her brand is stocked by prestigious retailers worldwide, and she has also collaborated with industry greats including Moncler and Nike, demonstrating how her work bridges high-end fashion and sportswear, a fundamental aspect of Japanese street- and sportswear.

A model walks the runway during Chitose Abe's
Spring/Summer 2017 show for Sacai, held in Paris.

Tao Kurihara, another Watanabe and Comme veteran but
educated at Central Saint Martins in London, launched
her eponymous brand in 2005. Her collections were often
heavily themed and would range from punk one season to
1980s aerobics gear the next. She only ever showed to a small
intimate audience, but the respect and critical acclaim she
attracted ensured her position as fashion maverick. While she
closed her label in 2011, and returned to Comme, the brand
is remembered for being a pioneer in what is now referred

to as upcycling. Kurihara crafted trench coats out of found handkerchiefs and stoles out of bedsheets. One of her final collections featured garments made out of carefully pleated white paper, a gentle nod to the Japanese craft of origami.

Also in 2005, Matohu was launched by design duo Hiroyuki Horihata and Makiko Sekiguchi. *Matohu* is a Japanese verb that expresses "softly wear", a term usually reserved for when wearing the kimono. The brand's name hints at its ethos, which has remained largely unchanged since its inception: the communication and appreciation of Japanese culture, traditions and concepts to an international audience in a modern and relevant way. To this end the duo has taken inspiration from the aesthetics of several important periods in Japanese history, but has also based entire collections on inherently Japanese concepts such as *nagori* – literally "remains of the waves", referring to what is left on the sand when the tide withdraws. It means the appreciation of the ephemeral and things that will end. Stylistically this ethos results in collections of elegant modern relaxed tailoring that demonstrate the universal relevance, possibilities and application of Japanese cultural concepts to the sphere of fashion.

A similar conceptual idea underpins Mint Designs, launched in 2001 by two more Central Saint Martins graduates, Hokuto Katsui and Nao Yagi. On their website, they write that they conceive of clothing as "a form of timeless product design that is not limited to the category of fashion. It is an item to enrich people's daily lives and sight" – an idea that chimes with several Japanese cultural practices.

This means they have consciously avoided trend-based collections and instead produce coherent thematic

Tokyo's Influence On The World

A model on the runway at Tao Kurihara's show for Spring/Summer 2010.

collections that show an independent design character and present a well-researched theme that has been extensively explored. Their aesthetic range has been extensive and evidences complex tailoring and production techniques, a commitment to textile innovation and an understanding of both Western and Japanese fashion history.

Another designer praised for her shunning of trends in favour of a wholly individual approach and aesthetic is Tamae Hirokawa of SOMARTA. She attended Bunka Fashion College and joined Issey Miyake after graduating. In 2006, Hirokawa created SOMA DESIGN, her own design company, and started working on multiple different projects spanning fashion, sound and graphic design. The SOMARTA fashion label was launched and quickly became an industry heavyweight. Unlike many of her predecessors and contemporaries, she shunned functionality and restraint in favour of expressive and often arresting conceptual design. Her clothes fuse conceptual aesthetics with futuristic textile technology, the result being both innovative and luxurious.

More recently, Kei Ninomiya's brand Noir deservedly joined the list of influential Japanese designers who continue to revitalize and challenge the industry. Ninomiya studied French literature at Aoyama University in Tokyo and later attended the Royal Academy of Fine Arts in Antwerp. Under the mentorship of Rei Kawakubo, he launched Noir in 2016. His often arresting, larger-than-life designs blur the boundaries between art and fashion. The result is often otherworldly, with garments resembling wearable sculptures. Like many of his predecessors, Ninomiya's work is characterized by innovative use of materials and futuristic technology. His juxtaposition of fabrics and textures results in artfully conceived, often traditionally feminine silhouettes that are always marked by a darker, more punkish undertone. His highly technologically complex 3D silhouettes not only

A model on the runway at the Matohu show in a silhouette that subtly hints at traditional Japanese dress culture in both cut and fabric design. Tokyo 2014.

carry on his spiritual design mother's ethos but arguably elevate it to new heights through the development of themes and concepts relevant to contemporary life.

As stated at the outset, this list of new creatives is hardly complete, but it is perhaps not an attempt to compile a roll call that matters so much as drawing attention to the fact that Japanese designers remain at the forefront of conceptual avant-garde design, continuing to revitalize the industry by standing as true innovators where so many are now followers.

A model wearing a design by Tamae Hirokawa for SOMARTA Spring/Summer 2008. The make-up is a modern interpretation of traditional kabuki face paint.

A model in a sculptural creation by Noir Kei Ninomiya,
Autumn/Winter 2020–21, held in Paris.

iNDEX

CREDITS

The publishers would like to thank the following sources for their kind permission to reproduce the pictures in this book.

(c) web-across.com by PARCO CO, LTD: 90, 91, 94, 114

Alamy: CPA Media Pte Ltd 34; Horst Friedrichs 125; Jack Malipan Travel Photography 140; Keystone Press 55; Meiji Showa 36; Science History Images 21

Bridgeman Images: © Brooklyn Museum of Art / Brooklyn Museum Libraries, Special Collections 26; © Dee Conway 107; Photo © Christie's Images 24; Photograph © 2022 Museum of Fine Arts, Boston. All rights reserved./ William Sturgis Bigelow Collection 15; Roy Miles Fine Paintings 18

Camera Press: Anthea Simms 66

Image Courtesy Fruits Magazine, Japan: 116, 117, 120, 123, 131

Getty Images: AFP 51; The Asahi Shimbun 50, 59, 81, 82, 84, 87, 95, 112; Barney Burstein 16; Chicago History Museum 42; Charles Phelps Cushing 39; Estrop: 147, 157; Evans 38; Fotosearch 23; Seeberger Freres 27; Gamma-Rapho 85; Herve Gloaguen 88; Pierre Guillaud 11; Koji Hirano 155; Hulton Deutsch 57; Images Press 105; Indianapolis Museum of Art at Newfields 43; Roger Jackson 54; Koichi Kamoshida 156; Onnie A Koski 136r; Gregory Pace 148; Pictures from History 33, 35; PYMCA 139; Jean-Claude Sauer 46; Sepia Times 19, 30, 32; Alex Serge 142; Daniel Simon 8, 53, 62, 70, 73, 76, 102; Matthew Sperzel 10, 132, 133, 136l, 143; Yoshikazu Tsuno 119; Pierre Vauthey 49, 93, Pierre Verdy 99; Victor Virgile 151; WWD 152; Bernard Weil 77

Kerry Taylor Auctions: 65, 68, 72, 74, 101, 106

MUJI: © Ryohin Keikaku Co., Ltd 7

Shutterstock: ANL 108; Chris Barham/ ANL 40; Roy Garner 126-127; Paul Harnett 135; Jean Jacques Levy/AP 52; Ilpo Musto 58; Eileen Tweedy 22

Topfoto: Heritage-Images 37

Every effort has been made to acknowledge correctly and contact the source and/or copyright holder of each picture and Welbeck Publishing apologises for any unintentional errors or omissions, which will be corrected in future editions of this book.